HERE COMES
FOOTBALL

A KIDS' GUIDE TO THE GAME

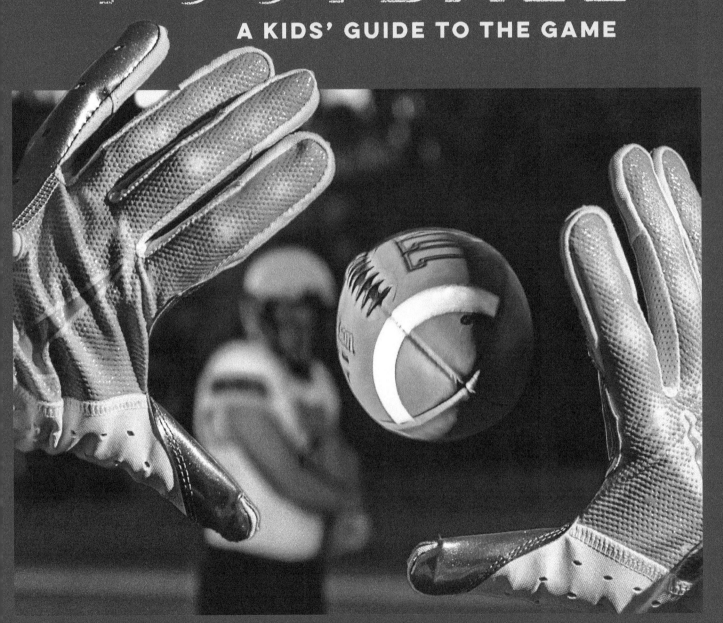

BURKLEY HOOVER

MISSION POINT PRESS

MISSION POINT PRESS

Published by Mission Point Press
2554 Chandler Rd.
Traverse City, MI 49696
(231) 421-9513
www.MissionPointPress.com

Design by Sarah Meiers

Cover photo by Will and Nicki Griffith.

ISBN 978-1-958363-45-4 (hardcover)
ISBN 978-1-958363-48-5 (softcover)

Library of Congress
Control Number 2022919451

Printed in the
United States of America

PHOTO COURTESY OF NICKI
GRIFFITH PHOTOGRAPHY

TABLE OF CONTENTS

PHOTO COURTESY OF NICKI GRIFFITH PHOTOGRAPHY

INTRODUCTION

I started writing this book for fun, but ended up learning a lot, like how a huddle started, the history of the game and how important it is for athletes to play many sports, not just one.

My dad inspired me to write this book. I get to watch him coach many awesome athletes. My family loves going to his games together.

When I asked my dad why he wanted to be a coach he said, "Because kids need a chance to chase their dreams. Kids just need someone to believe in them and to show them how to achieve their goals. I was lucky growing up. I had coaches that cared about me and my teammates so I think deep down it's my way of paying it forward."

ALL KIDS—BOYS AND GIRLS—CAN LOVE AND PLAY FOOTBALL.

I hope every kid learns something from this book and enjoys it with family and friends.

Burkley

FOREWORD

At her best, America is a diverse collection of souls, goals and shared love. The closest we get to see this model in action on a day-to-day basis is the Armed Forces and sports. And nowhere, in America (or anywhere else on this planet), do souls, goals and shared love intersect like they do in football.

It's a family affair.

A thousand years from now, scientists or aliens will see our football stadiums, towering and wrapped around fields, packing 100,000 area citizens, of all races and backgrounds *together*. Their research will show that those crowds were cheering, screaming and willing teams of all races and backgrounds who are striving and struggling, *together*.

Their souls, all indebted to the mission; their goals, all (for one night or a season) perfectly aligned; and their shared love of each other and their community, powering them through any obstacle. *Together*.

You see, America, for nearly a century, has had a working model on display on Fridays, Saturdays and Sundays for all to see, and even learn from. Football.

This perspective, from a young, wide-eyed author, who is growing up as a coach's kid, will translate to barbershops, synagogues, break rooms, trading floors, senior homes and surf shops with a television in them. Football touches us all.

Thanks to efforts like this one from Burkley Hoover, it will continue to inspire us all.

George Whitfield Jr.
Private Quarterback Coach
Founder, Whitfield Athletix

ACKNOWLEDGEMENTS

There are many people who made this book possible. At first, this project was just something I did for fun, but my friend, Tim Grunhard, believed in me and connected me with David Smale, who has helped me from beginning to end with this book. I would not have finished this book without him.

Thank you to my dad, who coaches football and made me love the sport. You inspire me and always encourage me to do my best and to try hard in all I do. And to my mom and sister, who always believe in me.

Many players and coaches helped me with interviews. Thank you for taking the time to answer my questions. It was so fun to learn your stories and tips that we can all use to be better teammates and players.

In my family we say, **"PLAY HARD AND HAVE FUN!"** I hope that's what all the readers will do.

Burkley

CHAPTER 1:
FOOTBALL HISTORY

WALTER CAMP invented football. He was a captain on the rugby team at Yale.

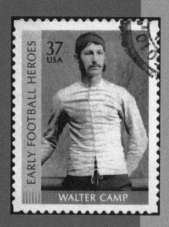

EARLY FOOTBALL HEROES
37 USA
WALTER CAMP

The first game played was in New Brunswick, New Jersey, on November 6, 1869. The first teams were Rutgers vs. Princeton, two college teams. College football started almost 50 years before professional football.

There are a few **DIFFERENCES** between rugby and football. You can only have 11 players on the field for football; in rugby, you have 15 players on the field. In rugby, players are required to wear a mouth guard. But in football, helmets and pads must be worn. The way the teams score in both rugby and football is similar. In football, players try and get the ball beyond the opponent's goal line. In rugby, players try to place the ball on the opponent's touch line.

Walter Camp made **NEW RULES** in 1880 that made the game more like the game we see on TV today. William "Pudge" Heffelfinger was paid $500 (about the same as $16,000 today) to play in a game on November 12, 1892, making him the first professional player.

The **NFL** was founded in September 1920 in Canton Ohio. There were originally 14 teams from 13 towns: five in Ohio, four in Illinois, and two in Indiana and New York.

The Arizona Cardinals and the Chicago Bears are the only two teams left from the **ORIGINAL TEAMS**. The Chicago Bears were originally the Decatur Staleys and the Arizona Cardinals were originally the Racine Street Cardinals. The Green Bay Packers, who played their first game in 1919, joined the NFL in the second season.

Some of the best football players had to fight in **WORLD WAR II**. When the war ended in 1945, gigantic numbers of athletic men were returning from military service. People had more money to spend, and they started showing games on TV to build excitement.

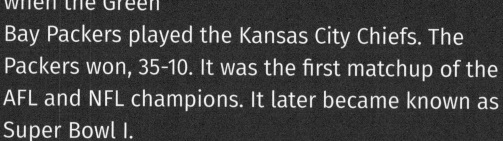

The first **SUPER BOWL** was played in Los Angeles on January 15, 1967, when the Green Bay Packers played the Kansas City Chiefs. The Packers won, 35-10. It was the first matchup of the AFL and NFL champions. It later became known as Super Bowl I.

The first **PRO BOWL** was played in January 1951. The Pro Bowl is the NFL's version of an all-star game. The Pro Bowl, the matchup between the best NFC players and best AFC players, is played the Sunday before the Super Bowl. The players are selected by the coaches, players and fans. The players who are selected but whose teams make it to the Super Bowl are not allowed to play in the Pro Bowl.

The **NFL** and **AFL** came together in 1970 and created the NFL we know today. The NFL is separated into two conferences: the AFC and the NFC.

Today the NFL is **HEADQUARTERED** in New York City and the Hall of Fame is in Canton, Ohio. You can take online tours of them.

CHAPTER 2

RULES

Here are some basic rules for the game.

FIRST DOWN. Teams get four downs to gain 10 yards. On fourth down, teams can either punt or go for it and try to get the first down. If they get the first down, they keep playing on offense. If they do not get the first down, the other team gets the ball where the offensive team had it.

FIELD GOAL. A field goal is worth three points. The offense can choose to attempt a field goal from anywhere or at any time. Usually teams try a field goal on fourth down, unless the team thinks they can get a first down or a touchdown.

EXTRA POINT. This point is made after the offense scores a touchdown. It is worth one point. The offense can also go for a two-point conversion after a touchdown instead of kicking the extra point. Sometimes teams will try a trick play. The ball is placed at the 3-yard line for college and high school, and the 2-yard line for the pros. The offense stays on the field and runs a normal play for two points. In the NFL, if a team elects to kick the extra point, the ball is placed at the 15-yard line.

FORWARD PASS. Knute Rockne invented the forward pass. The first forward pass in a game was on September 5, 1906. Bradbury Robinson threw the ball to Jack Schneider at St. Louis University. A forward pass is a pass thrown from behind the line of scrimmage in a forward direction, toward the opponent's goal.

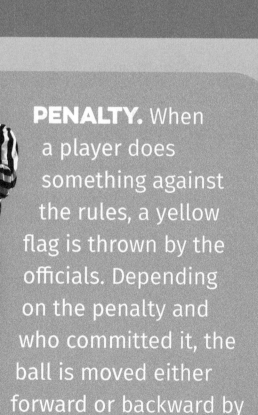

PENALTY. When a player does something against the rules, a yellow flag is thrown by the officials. Depending on the penalty and who committed it, the ball is moved either forward or backward by 5, 10 or 15 yards.

PARTICIPATION. Teams must have 11 players on the field; if they have more than 11 players they get a penalty.

OVERTIME. Overtime happens when the teams are tied at the end of the game and there is no more time left in the game. Overtime is an extra period.

The overtime rules are different in college and the NFL. **IN THE NFL,** there is a coin-flip to see who gets the ball first. In the regular season, there can be no more than one 10-minute period. If the team that gets the ball first scores a touchdown, they win. Otherwise, the other team gets a chance to score. In 2022, the NFL changed its overtime rules for the playoffs. Now each team gets the ball no matter what.

IN COLLEGE, each team gets a chance to score and there is no time limit. If teams are still tied after the first overtime, they must try a 2-point conversion for all remaining overtimes. The overtime keeps going until one team leads after both teams end their possession.

CHAPTER 3:
GEAR & EQUIPMENT

In 1888, the college football rules convention voted to allow tackling below the waist. Players and coaches soon regarded pads as essential for the game. Equipment is important to the game of football. There have been a lot of changes throughout the years.

The first **FOOTBALL HELMETS**, called "head harnesses," were made out of leather. Between 1915 and 1917, the first full head protection was introduced. Helmets became mandatory in 1939. Riddell company invented the plastic helmet in the 1940s.

The first set of **SHOULDER PADS** were made for extra protection by LP Smock (a Princeton student) in 1877. **CLEATS**, the shoes players wear to give them better grip on the field, have been around since the beginning of football. In football, the pants have a built-in padding system for knees, thighs, hips and the tailbone. In pro football, the jerseys are numbered based on the position of each player.

In the 1900s the equipment started to get better to keep players safer from injury.

1920s: the first hardened helmets and leather pads were introduced.

1930s: foam pads and facemasks were added to helmets.

1940s: chinstraps were added to helmets and the first leather shoulder pads were used.

1950s AND 1960s: helmets started being made out of padded plastic. The American Dental Association began explaining how mouthguards help protect players. By 1962 all high school football players had to wear a mouthguard.

1960s AND 1970s: football players began using reinforced plastic pads.

We have learned a lot about player safety. Equipment companies are always trying to make better equipment to keep players safe. That is very important, because the players have gotten much bigger, faster and stronger over time.

EQUIPMENT MANAGERS are also a very important part of the team, because they take care of all the equipment, like jerseys, helmets, pants, pads, cleats, mouth guards and more. They make sure the equipment makes it to every game, home and away.

Can you guess what the most important piece of equipment is? If you guessed the **FOOTBALL**, then you are correct! There would not be a game of football without the ball.

People call the football "pigskin," but today it is actually made of cowhide. In the 1800s, the football was made of a pig's skin and bladder, which is where the nickname "pigskin" came from. The shape of a football is actually a similar shape to a pig's bladder.

RADIOS are used in NFL helmets for quarterbacks and one player on defense on each team, which helps make communication from coaches to players in the huddle easier.

GLOVES originally were worn to keep players' hands warm, but they have become a normal accessory for almost all positions. They help skill-position players grip the football better, and help linemen protect their hands.

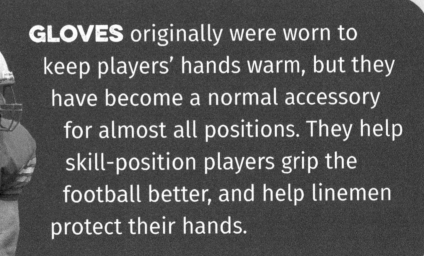

CHAPTER 4:
BIG NAMES
AND GREAT TEAMS

Current and Recent Stars

TOM BRADY is a quarterback. He has won six Super Bowls with the New England Patriots and one with the Tampa Bay Buccaneers. The quarterback is the leader, and Brady is considered one of the greatest quarterbacks of all time.

BRUCE SMITH was a defensive end and is the NFL's all-time sack leader. Smith was picked for the Pro Bowl 11 times and had 200 career sacks. A sack is when you tackle the quarterback behind the line of scrimmage.

EMMITT SMITH was a running back for the Dallas Cowboys and Arizona Cardinals. The three-time Super Bowl champion is also the NFL's all-time leader in rushing yards and touchdowns. Running backs don't just run the ball. They catch, block and sometimes even throw.

JERRY RICE, nicknamed "World" for his amazing catching ability, was a wide receiver for 20 seasons in the NFL (the most ever at that position). He had an NFL record 1,549 career catches. Rice proved you do not have to be the fastest runner to be a great wide receiver.

PATRICK MAHOMES plays quarterback for the Kansas City Chiefs. In 2018, he threw for more than 5,000 yards, which made him the only quarterback in history to throw that many yards in both college and the NFL. He is the youngest quarterback to win the Most Valuable Player in the Super Bowl. Mahomes played baseball and football while attending Texas Tech University. He will be fun to watch for seasons to come.

JAMIE SQUIRE/GETTY IMAGES

Early stars

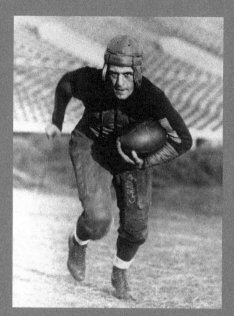

HAROLD "RED" GRANGE was nicknamed "The Galloping Ghost." He went to Illinois and played halfback. He was a three-time all-American. He took his team to the national championship in 1923. He joined the Bears in 1925. He was voted the best college player of all time by ESPN.

OTTO GRAHAM was a quarterback for the Cleveland Browns. When Graham was quarterback, he held the longest winning streak. He entered Northwestern University in 1940 on a basketball scholarship. Later football became his main sport.

ELROY HIRSCH was a halfback who got inducted into the Pro Football Hall of Fame in 1967 and the College Football Hall of Fame in 1974. He was nicknamed "Crazylegs" because of his unusual running style in which his legs twisted as he ran. He was the general manager for the Los Angeles Rams for nine years, and the athletic director for Wisconsin for 15 years.

JOHNNY UNITAS was a Hall of Fame and MVP-winning quarterback. Unitas played most of his career for the Baltimore Colts. Originally drafted in the ninth round, he was cut immediately by the Pittsburgh Steelers and was barely paid to play football, before the Colts took a chance on him. He went on to play 18 seasons in the NFL.

LEN DAWSON played pro football for 19 seasons, most of them for the Kansas City Chiefs. He played quarterback, and his teammates called him "Lenny The Cool." He still held seven Chiefs career records, including passing yards, as the 2022 season began.

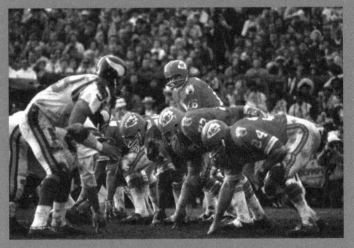

DICK BUTKUS was one of the most talented linebackers to play the game. Butkus played for the Chicago Bears and was a two-time all-American in college. He was the third overall pick in 1965, and he had 22 interceptions and 27 fumble recoveries.

Coaches

GEORGE HALAS coached football for 40 seasons. He also played football, and played Major League Baseball for the New York Yankees. He was one of the oldest people in NFL history to be a head coach. He was inducted into the Pro Football Hall of Fame.

JOHN MADDEN was a Super Bowl-winning coach for the Oakland Raiders. He also played offensive tackle for a short amount of time for the Philadelphia Eagles. Madden is also famous for a video game called "Madden NFL" that was first made in 1988 and has sold more than 100 million copies. Madden is not the most successful coach, but he is one of the best-known. He was also a great broadcaster, and Madden NFL is a very popular video game.

BETTMANN/GETTY IMAGES

The winningest coach in NFL history is **DON SHULA** with 328 wins. Second is Bill Belichick, who has the most wins among active coaches. Next on the active list is Andy Reid, the coach of the Kansas City Chiefs who was the coach of the Philadelphia Eagles from 2001 to 2012.

EDDIE ROBINSON was the head coach at Grambling State, a Historically Black College and University (HBCU), from 1941-1997. He was inducted into the College Football Hall of Fame in 1997. He turned Grambling State into a college football powerhouse during a period of time when Black players were not allowed to play for most schools in the south.

NICK SABAN is one of the winningest college football coaches. He has won national championships at LSU and Alabama. Saban also was an assistant coach and head coach in the NFL. Saban has won more games than any other active Division I coach.

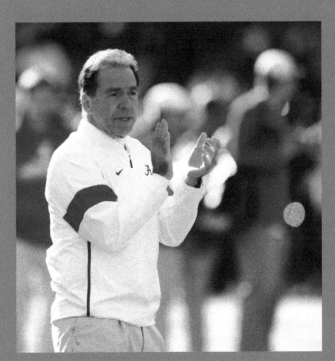

KEVIN C. COX/GETTY IMAGES

Teams

The **NEW ENGLAND PATRIOTS** and **PITTSBURGH STEELERS** are tied with six Super Bowl wins. No team in the NFL has appeared in more Super Bowls than the Patriots (11). In the 2000s, the Patriots were dominant with head coach Bill Belichick and quarterback Tom Brady.

The **GREEN BAY PACKERS** are the third oldest franchise in the NFL. The Packers are owned by a unique combination of their season ticket holders, fans and citizens of the town of Green Bay, Wisc. They play their home games in Lambeau Field. A tradition of the Packers is the "Lambeau Leap," where players jump into the stands as a part of their touchdown celebration.

In 1972, the **MIAMI DOLPHINS** went undefeated during the regular season and playoffs and are still the only team in the Super Bowl era to have a perfect (undefeated) season.

The **DALLAS COWBOYS** are known as "America's Team." They were really bad in 1989 (1-15) before winning three Super Bowls in four years. They were led by three of the league's biggest stars: Troy Aikman (QB), Emmitt Smith (RB) & Michael Irvin (WR).

In 1998, the **DENVER BRONCOS** won their second straight Super Bowl. Hall of Fame quarterback John Elway retired after 16 years in the NFL. The Broncos are one of only seven teams to win back-to-back (in a row) Super Bowls.

The **KANSAS CITY CHIEFS,** led by star quarterback Patrick Mahomes, have hosted a record four straight conference championship games (following the 2018-21 seasons) and won the Super Bowl in 2020.

CHAPTER 5:

TIPS FROM THE PROS

Coaches

NFL
MIKE VRABEL, TENNESSEE TITANS

How do you stay so focused and calm when your team is losing or it is a tight score?

VRABEL: "By focusing on the next play and not on past mistakes. Things can change and you can always turn things around."

SILAS WALKER/GETTY IMAGES

What is the most difficult part about being a coach?

VRABEL: "Being away from your family and the sacrifice the family has to make because of your commitment to the team. When players make mistakes after you've worked so hard it can be frustrating sometimes."

What is the coolest thing about being a coach?

VRABEL: "Watching players grow, improve and see the reward for the time that everyone has put in together. It's cool to see the players excited about coming to work every day and working hard because they love football."

Would you rather win a Super Bowl as a coach or a player?

VRABEL: "When I win one as a coach, I think it will be more rewarding than winning one as a player. Because I was able to win as a player, I know how special it is and I think it will be more rewarding to share that with a group of players."

MARCUS FREEMAN, UNIVERSITY OF NOTRE DAME

NOTRE DAME ATHLETICS

What are you looking for in a player you recruit?

FREEMAN: "I'm always looking for what I refer to as CATIL: Competitive, Athletic, Tough, Intelligent, Leaders, in that order.

Is Gameday your favorite day of the week?

FREEMAN: "Yes. I love Saturdays. Each day of the week builds in anticipation to Saturdays. It's the day you work so hard for each week.

Do you like to recruit players who are multi-sport athletes or ones that focus year round on football?

FREEMAN: "I prefer to recruit multi-sport athletes. I love when athletes pick up multiple skill sets. It makes them more well-rounded overall. You can also see recruits compete in many different aspects and not just see them competing against themselves in training.

What is the best part of your job?

FREEMAN: "The best part of my job is seeing our players reach their goals. At the end of the day, the entire purpose of this position, in my opinion, is helping the players in our program reach all of their goals. When they do achieve that success, there is no greater satisfaction for me.

HIGH SCHOOL

TRENT DILFER, SUPER BOWL-WINNING QUARTERBACK WITH THE BALTIMORE RAVENS IN 2000, HEAD FOOTBALL COACH AT LIPSCOMB ACADEMY IN NASHVILLE, TENN.

What made you want to coach after a long playing career and being on TV?

DILFER: "I wanted to give back and share all of the things I had learned through my career and help as many players as I can."

How do you motivate the players when things aren't going well?

DILFER: "First, you have to earn their trust. Then when things aren't going well, they know they can trust you and are motivated because they know you have good advice for them."

You won a Super Bowl as a player and a state championship as a coach. How do they compare?

DILFER: "Winning a Super Bowl was a relief, but winning a state championship was more satisfying. It was so fun to see the joy from the players and coaches."

Do you prefer throwing a touchdown or calling a play for a touchdown?

DILFER: "I still like throwing touchdowns more, because I wish I would have thrown more. It's very hard to throw touchdowns."

Players

QUARTERBACK
DREW LOCK, SEATTLE SEAHAWKS

What are some warm-up drills that you like to do to warm up your arm?

LOCK: "I start with short throws (5-10 yards apart) that work on rotation and follow-through."

Did you play any other sports or did you play any other positions in football?

LOCK: "I played mostly basketball growing up. Playing other sports made me a better athlete and competitor. Just like seeing the field in football, basketball helped me see the court and who was open."

What is your favorite part of being a QB?

LOCK: "I like being in control, and I like the responsibility of the team counting on me to win or lose."

What is the hardest thing about being a QB in the NFL?

LOCK: "More than the players being big and fast, it's really how smart all of the players are on defense."

OFFENSIVE LINE
TIM GRUNHARD, FORMER KANSAS CITY CHIEFS CENTER

What are some warm-up drills you liked to do before a game?

GRUNHARD: "I think every position should have a different warm-up drill, because every position uses different muscles. I went to the goal post, 'chopped my feet,' and worked on the pass-set-punch. Stretching is really important, because it warms you up. You are only as good as you warm up your body to be."

Did you get hurt a lot while you were playing?

GRUNHARD: "There's a difference between pain and injury. When you are injured, you can't play. But you can play through some pain. Pain and hurt are part of the game for all sports."

Did you play any other positions or sports growing up?

GRUNHARD: "Yes, the more sports you play growing up the better for an athlete and competitor. Then, as you get older, you can start to figure out what you are good at and focus more on those."

What is your favorite part about playing center?

GRUNHARD: "Being in charge, being a leader and helping the other players or teammates with their responsibilities. Much like the quarterback, you have to know what everyone on the field is doing."

What is the hardest thing about being an offensive lineman?

GRUNHARD: "It's hard work. You don't get to score touchdowns, but you feel great watching a teammate score and you know it's because of a block you made."

RUNNING BACK
NATRONE MEANS, FORMER SAN DIEGO CHARGERS RUNNING BACK

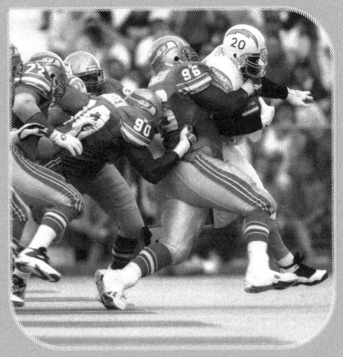

What skill was most difficult in your position?

MEANS: "Blocking. Running the ball was easy for me, but being able to protect the quarterback was difficult and required the most work because it's technical."

Did you play any other sports?

MEANS: "I played multiple sports. I played football, basketball, baseball and track. The other sports always helped me improve in football too. They all require running, jumping, cutting, etc., and it always helped that I competed year round."

What did you do to warm up?

MEANS: "Break a sweat, high knees, skips and dynamic warmups because running backs have to make sharp cuts and you need your feet and ankles loose and ready."

RECEIVER
TYLER LOCKETT, RECEIVER, SEATTLE SEAHAWKS

JUSTIN CASTERLINE/GETTY IMAGES

How do you focus on catching the ball and running at the same time?

LOCKETT: "There are a lot of things we do in our everyday life that require us to do two things at once. At the end of the day you learn to focus on catching and running by getting very good at both of them. Then it becomes easier to do them at the same time."

Do you have any tips for how you can practice catching without a QB?

LOCKETT: "I like to juggle tennis balls, golf balls (anything smaller than a football) to work on focus and hand-eye coordination. You aren't always going to have a QB available."

How do you fake out defenders in order to get open?

LOCKETT: "It's all about illusion. Show the defender something different than the direction you are planning on going. Learn body control so you can change direction without losing speed."

DEFENSIVE LINE
SOLOMON THOMAS, DEFENSIVE TACKLE, NEW YORK JETS (THIRD OVERALL PICK BY THE SAN FRANCISCO 49ERS IN 2017)

Was football always your favorite sport?

THOMAS: "Football was not always my favorite. My dad was a big basketball player and I loved shooting hoops with him and having him coach me. So basketball was my favorite sport."

Did you play any other sports? If so, how did they help you with football?

THOMAS: "I played basketball, football, track and lacrosse, and I was also a swimmer. Track helped me learn to be fast and make cuts. Lacrosse helped me be physical, and basketball probably helped me the most being able to change direction on a dime, plyometrics and understanding body positions. And swimming helped me with my cardio and stamina."

As a defensive lineman, what is one thing you have to do to be good at your job?

THOMAS: "I think your hands are the most important. You have to have good hand placement, violent hands and hand structure."

Since defensive lineman try to sack the quarterback, who is your favorite quarterback to sack so far?

THOMAS: "Sacking Ben Roethlisberger was a huge moment for me because he is a (future) Hall of Fame quarterback and I've been watching him since I was a kid."

LINEBACKER
WILLIE MCGINEST, FORMER LINEBACKER WITH THE NEW ENGLAND PATRIOTS

MITCHELL LAYTON/GETTY IMAGES

Did you like being the leader of the defense?

McGINEST: "Leading by example and always being willing to do whatever you would ask of someone else are important parts of being a leader. Leadership comes in many forms. You can show people, talk to people or make sacrifices for the team. But mainly, it's being willing to do whatever is best for the team, even if that changes over time. 'Team over individual' is important. I worked hard without people telling me to do it. Leadership is putting the team above yourself."

How did you practice paying attention to snap counts and cadence each week?

McGINEST: "I always listened for cadence and snap counts. Any edge you can get defensively, you take it. During practice, we listened to TV sound, looked at hand and foot movements, which foot was forward, looked at any motion by the quarterback when under center, etc. Anything to give us an edge."

Did you set goals to break records, or did it just happen by playing hard?

McGINEST: "I had goals to be the best player I could be, but I never set goals to break a certain record. I focused on what I needed to do and then they happened."

Was the blitz the most fun part of your job?

McGINEST: "It was definitely one of my favorite parts, but it was just one of many parts of the job. My position was very versatile and sometimes required dropping back for coverage instead of going after the quarterback."

DEFENSIVE BACK
RAY MICKENS PLAYED 11 SEASONS IN THE NFL, MAINLY FOR THE NEW YORK JETS

What is a warm-up drill you did to get ready for games?

MICKENS: "I liked to do a lot of drills that would get my lower body warmed up, including shuffling, backpedaling and zig-zag running."

Did you like making big hits or interceptions more?

MICKENS: "I liked making interceptions more than big hits because big hits sometimes hurt us both. One of my nicknames was 'Big Play Ray' for my big plays I made on the ball."

Did you like playing in college or the NFL more?

MICKENS: "I liked playing in college more because I was able to spend a lot of time with my teammates. You live in the dorms together and have class with other students on campus so the fans in college make it a special experience."

What is some advice you would give to a kid like me that is just learning to play football?

MICKENS: "Have fun, learn the fundamentals and the third rule is to remind yourself to have fun. Sometimes as a competitor it's hard to do that when things aren't going exactly like you want them to."

CHAPTER 6

FUN FACTS

Every NFL football since 1955 has been made in the **WILSON FACTORY** in Ada, Ohio. They produce more than 700,000 footballs each year.

The Tampa Bay Buccaneers and the Los Angeles Rams both played the Super Bowl in their own **STADIUMS**. It had never happened before Super Bowl LV (in January 2021), but it has happened twice in a row! (And they both won!)

SARAH FULLER became the first woman to play in a college football game when she played for Vanderbilt. She wore number 32 on her jersey. On the back of her helmet, it said "Play like a girl." After a game, she said, "I just want to tell all the girls out there that you can do anything you set your mind to."

Currently there are **TWO WOMEN WORKING AS REFEREES** in the NFL, with many more training and working at other levels of football.

Notre Dame **REPAINTS** their helmets gold before each game!

The **HEISMAN TROPHY** is given to the "most outstanding player in college football." Did you know only one player has ever won the trophy twice? It was Archie Griffin from Ohio State in 1974 and 1975. Players from Ohio State and Notre Dame have won seven each.

The **TWO COUNTRIES** where American football is most popular are Canada and the United States. Canadian football allows 12 players on the field at one time, while in the United States they have 11 players on the field. In Canada, the football field is 110 yards long, while in the United States it is 100 yards. That is a 10-yard difference!

Not every football team in the NFL has **CHEERLEADERS**. When the Green Bay Packers and the Pittsburgh Steelers played in Super Bowl XLV, it became the first Super Bowl where there were no cheerleaders on either sideline!

The huddle started with **TWO DEAF TEAMS**. In 1894, the quarterback for Gallaudet, Paul Hubbard, thought the other team was going to see their plays while using sign language on the field. So he created a "group circle" with his teammates. That is how the huddle was created. This is how teams communicate when they need to share a play, though they use signals when stadiums are loud or they want to hurry the pace.

The quarterback uses a **RHYTHM** to communicate with his or her teammates to tell them when the center is going to snap the ball. That is called "the cadence." The defense doesn't have any idea what that cadence is. It is basically a secret language.

GLOSSARY

SACK: when the quarterback is tackled behind the line of scrimmage.

OFFICIALS: the seven people in charge of calling the game and making sure both teams follow the rules.

FUMBLE: when a player loses possession of the ball.

BLOCK: a technique used by the team with the ball to keep the tacklers away from the ball carrier by pushing and moving their feet.

INTERCEPTION: when the quarterback throws the ball and a defender catches it.

TACKLE: when you take the player with the ball to the ground.

BLITZ: when an extra linebacker, safety or cornerback tries to pounce on the quarterback. A blitz usually has five or more defenders rushing.

L.O.S. (Line of scrimmage): the yard line that the ball is on.

TAILGATING: an activity before the game where people eat food, play games and get ready to cheer on their teams.

POCKET: the area in the backfield that is formed by the offensive line and where the quarterback wants to throw from.

SNAP COUNT: the cadence that the offense uses to tell the center when to snap the ball to begin the play.

SCRAMBLE: when the quarterback runs to get away from the defense.

PUNT: a kick that happens by the offensive team when they do not get a touchdown or first down.

LATERAL: a backwards pass.

R.P.O. (Run/Pass/Option): the quarterback has the option to hand off or throw depending on what the defense does.

PLAY-ACTION: a type of play that looks like a run to the defense but is actually a designed pass.

FLEA FLICKER: a play the offense runs to try and trick the defense.

TOUCHBACK: a kick or punt that goes into the endzone that the receiving team decides not to return.

NFL (National Football League): the NFL has 32 teams that play on television. Most games are played on Sundays, but there are also games on Thursdays and Mondays.

ABOUT THE AUTHOR

Burkley Hoover lives in Kansas City, Missouri. She was introduced to football by her dad. He is a quarterbacks coach, which makes it her favorite position in football.

She has one sister, Avery, who loves football just like Burkley does. Her mom loves taking them to games and cheering as loud as she can for their favorite teams and players.

Burkley plays a lot of sports, including volleyball, soccer, golf, basketball and swimming. She loves playing sports and reading books. Burkley wants to share her love of football with other kids and especially young girls.

Printed in the USA
CPSIA information can be obtained
at www.ICGtesting.com
LVHW071457171023
761360LV00003B/49